OUTSOURCE YOUR MVP

MATT KELLY
4TH EDITION

1

4th Edition
Copyright Matt Kelly 2015
Print and distribution: lulu.com
Digital distribution: amazon.com
Further information: mattkelly.com.au

OUTSOURCE YOUR MVP

ADVANCE PRAISE
OUTSOURCE YOUR MVP

This wise and insightful guide on how to outsource work, via the multitude of platforms available, will be of immediate value to Entrepreneurs. From using Virtual Assistants, right through to hiring a Web Designer and Developer to get a complete website built. Invest your time in this book and you will save a hundred hours later on because Matt tells all about what to expect and what many of the options are.

Simon Tannock
Scientist
Queensland, Australia

Matt Kelly is a pioneer in the outsourcing industry. He has laid out a realistic and fool-proof process to go about outsourcing. Matt's quick tips are ingenious, and the resources he lists in the book are key to any successful project. Simply put, Matt makes outsourcing a piece of cake for those who were beginners like me.

Crystal Ramjattan
Engineer and Entrepreneur
New York, United States of America

Whether you're working for the hourly rate, CEO of your own company or a busy 9-5 professional, trying to beat the rat race. The world is changing, and the old models and practices don't cut it. Matt has uncovered a bullet proof guide to ultimately maximize your productivity and increase your personal time. From, designing a website, to developing new product prototypes. A world of infinite options awaits for those who read this book. It is a manifesto and complete blueprint guide to outsourcing. Its a game changer and a must read!

Chris Baker
Author of The Six Figure Graduate
California, United States of America

Chapter 1: Let's Do It   8

Chapter 2: A History Lesson   21

Chapter 3: Validating Your Idea   23

Chapter 4: The Platforms   29

Chapter 5: Virtual Assistants   37

Chapter 6: Getting Your Requirements Down   40

Chapter 7: Writing The Brief   50

Chapter 8: Pricing Your Project   56

Chapter 9: Pulling The Trigger   63

Chapter 10: Managing The Project   66

Chapter 11: Close to Completion   69

Chapter 12: Pitfalls And Challenges   73

Chapter 13: Resources   76

Chapter 14: Bonus   78

A NOTE FROM THE AUTHOR

Over the past few years, I've worked on a range of digital projects which have included the creation of websites, blogs and apps; for myself, small business clients, large corporates, and not-for-profit organizations. I've worked with many designers and developers over the years, both locally in Australia and the United States of America (the places I call home), and to this day, I'm consistently amazed by the opportunities that have become available in recent years to outsource digital work.

I read recently that seventy-three percent of self-education products purchased online never get used; people download books and courses but don't take action. By reading this far, you're in the minority. If you have a passion or an idea, or you see an opportunity, don't let a lack of technical knowledge cause it to pass you by. Take note and make it happen!

Though outsourcing internationally comes with many pros and cons, it represents a huge opportunity for highly technically, capable, freelancers located all over the world to work with entrepreneurs with minimal investment.

While every effort has been made to ensure that the information in this book is reliable and current, you should exercise care and consideration when you attempt to utilize any of the websites, techniques, thoughts or strategies mentioned herein.

Please also note that when you engage freelancers from an emerging country, the nominal amount you will be paying will likely be less than you might pay a local agency. These suppliers are often relying on your payment for their livelihood, and while their cost of living may be far less than that of someone in a first world country you should always be responsible, pay a reasonable amount for the work done, and always pay on time.

Finally, I have nothing to gain from you outsourcing your project. I'm not typically a freelancer myself, I'm just someone that hopes that with your new found knowledge, you'll be empowered to bring your vision to fruition to improve the world.

If you've got an idea for a new website, blog, business or app, enjoy the read and I hope you'll consider giving a skilled worker freelancer a shot!

Kind regards,

Matthew Kelly
matt@mattkelly.com.au

THE DISCLAIMER

As this book is for educational purposes only, neither the author, narrator, nor any other party is responsible for any damages that may arise out of the use of the materials, regardless of whether they were consumed on a website, via email, this document, or any other associated format.

Be responsible: If you find this information valuable and relevant, and choose to take action, that's great, but remember that you hold the power to your destiny and any actions you take as a result of consuming any material in this book or on any affiliated medium are   of your own choosing.

I'm providing you with these stories, anecdotes and experiences in the hope that they inspire you, however any information documented should not be relied upon, trusted or even utilized. Every day we take calculated risks. I can't promise you won't be scammed on your first experience or that you won't end up with a product that's not up to scratch. Utilizing these tools come with challenges. I just want to share some of what I've learned in the hope that you may be better educated, prepared and will perhaps find value in utilizing some of this material for your next project.

CHAPTER 1: LET'S DO IT!

WELCOME

If you've reached this far, I'll go out on a limb and assume that it's quite likely I can sum you up in one line - you have some great ideas, and you're ready to execute! Was I right? You should only continue if you've made the decision to take action on getting your project live, and you're ready to go about building out your project in an exciting, rewarding, and sometimes even challenging way.

Outsourcing digitally is a powerful, and exciting way of complementing your current skill set to assist in the build phase of a project. Popular applications of digital outsourcing include:

- Designing and developing a website
- Building a blog
- Creating a mobile application
- Copywriting
- Utilizing a virtual assistant to deal with your administrative tasks
- Proofreading
- Modernizing or refreshing your website
- Adding mobile capability to your business' website
- Creating a piece of software
- Wire-framing or conceptualizing a new online page
- New product design
- Graphical mockups
- and many more.

After reading this book, I hope that you'll know all the basics required to outsource your project to an expert when you need a hand.

THE MVP

When this book was first published, it was titled 'The Entrepreneur's Guide To Outsourcing With Confidence'. As you might expect, upon writing the first edition, I had the thousands of business owners in mind who've build a company, and need help scaling quickly.

The truth is, I'm incredibly passionate about the startup industry. I enjoy nothing more than studying the development of new tech companies, assessing market value, watching ideas turn into platforms used by millions of people, and occasionally even seeing the big exit for millions (or billions) of dollars.

Historically (and by historically, we're really just talking about the past few years), you had to be an engineer, a designer, or a developer to build out a tech startup. While that's still a common belief, the reality is I've build dozens of web platforms (including a couple of fairly complex projects) as a non-technical founder   (read: not a web developer) with outsourced partners as my technology arm.

So while most assume that 'outsourcing' becomes valuable when you've built your product or website, and you need help replicating or systemizing processes, I've had a contrary experience. I primarily outsource when in the very early stages of a startup to validate an idea with a customer base, before investing thousands of dollars and hours into building. This is the process of the minimum viable product (commonly referred to as an MVP).

The minimum viable product, is a term that was coined by Steve Blank and Eric Ries, long time influencers in the tech industry. By modern definitions, your MVP is essentially a minimal, stripped back version of your product that can be built quickly, and put in the hands of your customers, which then enables you to assess whether you're truly solving a problem. If this early version of your product's core feature-set proves your hypothesis correct, you can build out a fuller more comprehensive version of your product with the confidence of knowing that you're solving a problem for your customers.

This goes against the trend of past, where businesses would invest thousands (even millions) of dollars to build a company behind closed doors, without ever really knowing whether their solution is right for their market (until it's too late of course).

By building a MVP, you're essentially taking your big vision, stripping it back, and building out the least amount of technology required to validate your thinking. This ultimately accelerates learning, reduces time and money, gets the product to customers quickly, to validate market need.

ACTIVITY

Use this space to draw, sketch or list the elements within your fully featured product, and then cross out all of the supplementary, or non-core features. This will help you to determine what needs to be included in your MVP, and will form the basis of your initial hypothesis.

ACTIVITY CONT.

How'd you go? If you included 'nice to have' features in your MVP, strip it back further. The core purpose of your MVP is to validate market need, nothing more.

OUTSOURCING DEFINED

In simple terms, outsourcing is the delegation of tasks to a third party. Theoretically, you can outsource work anywhere: to family, friends, a neighborhood small business, a digital agency, or even a large organization.

The Internet has bridged the gap for outsourcing work internationally. However, because the cost of living is significantly lower in some countries than others, it is often entirely possible to get work done by highly-skilled individuals for a fraction of the price you might pay locally.

By outsourcing tasks that are not specifically core to your organization, you'll have the opportunity to gain access to unique, affordable, and time-saving skills to give you a chance to focus your time, effort and money on doing what you do best (or what you prefer to do).

Both pros and cons exist. If you are the kind of person who enjoys walking into an office and talking to the person doing the work - and don't mind paying a premium to do so - perhaps this isn't for you. But if you are keen to learn about outsourcing, you know what result you want, and you are willing to put in the time, you may be able to get a unique and significantly less expensive result by outsourcing work all over the world. If you still aren't sure, remember that you have a range of powerful tools at your fingertips which enable audio calling, video conferencing and even screen sharing capability. In many cases, this is enough to build a solid relationship with your newfound developer on the other side of the world.

On a side note, your 'local *owned and operated* design agency' may actually be outsourcing all of its grunt work overseas as we speak, and simply acting as relationship manager to their end client. If you're looking to pay up to 20 times more for a relationship manager to run your project, that's fine, but if you're excited about taking control of your project, let's give it a go.

For the purpose of this book, the term 'outsourcing' relates to utilizing digital platforms to outsource your work to technology professionals all over the world.

I have outsourced both design and development, administration and marketing work (typically web projects), to professionals in countries like India, Philippines, China, Singapore, Finland, Serbia, Uzbekistan, India, Argentina and Romania.

Examples in this book, by default, will be about the development of websites, given that is one of the most common types of tasks being outsourced. However, in almost all cases, the same techniques and thought processes can be applied to any number of tasks. The only requirement is a little common sense.

Anywhere a dollar value is quoted, it can be assumed that this is in US currency.

QUICK TIP

Still not sure? Go and check out Skype and GoToMeeting and utilize these platforms to collaborate on jobs and create strong relationships.

OUTSOURCING VERSUS OFFSHORING

People often mix up the terms outsourcing and offshoring. The simple distinction: outsourcing typically relates to the contracting of a project or task to an external organization, whereas offshoring relates to explicitly having work completed by an external company in a different country, usually to take advantage of reduced costs. In short, you can outsource to an individual or organization in your own country. For this to be offshoring, the organization being contracted must be in a different country.

In many cases, if you outsource a task, you'll be both outsourcing and offshoring. However for others you may even find that it makes more sense for you to outsource a task to someone in your own country. There really isn't a right answer here, it all comes down to the specifics of the project.

THE KEY BENEFITS

By this stage, you probably don't need to be sold on the benefits of outsourcing your tasks to contractors all over the world. But in case you need just one more nudge, read on.

Lower costs

This is perhaps the number one reason people choose to outsource, a primary benefit. You can get work done at a fraction of the cost that you might need to spend locally (subject to where you are of course). As was mentioned earlier, the cost of living is significantly lower in emerging countries, where skilled workers don't need to charge inflated rates. Secondly, many of these people have created great efficiencies in the way they execute tasks. This enables significantly faster timeframes for execution, minimizing the total cost of a project. A web developer in an emerging country might charge between 10% and 30% of what a local developer may quote.

Are they good?

If you attended a university in a Western country, you know that it's entirely possible that 50% of your fellow students travelled from another country to study there. More and more students from emerging countries are studying at educational institutions in the West and returning home after completing their degree, diploma or certificate.

What does this result in? Well, if they learned the same skills as your local web designer, at the same university, and then traveled back to their homeland (where the cost to live is significantly lower), they can afford to undercut your local business owner while still delivering the same, or possibly even better results.

The clock

People often consider time difference to be a major outsourcing drawback. The truth is however, with some smarts this can be used as a huge advantage. How many of your competitors are developing and completing work twenty-four hours per day? Likely none.

Consider this: If you live in the USA and your outsourced web designer is in Asia - literally on the other side of the world - you can brief them on a project or provide feedback at the end of the day, which works out to being the start of their day. While you sleep, they'll be working. When you wake up, you've got a product to assess, you can provide additional feedback, and you can repeat the process. Talk about efficiency! You're literally getting work done while you sleep.

Keeping focused

At the end of the day, you really want to spend time focusing on the reason why you started your business in the first place. That reason could be to save time, make more money, live a particular lifestyle or make the world a better place. If you're able to remove the technical or administrative tasks from your workload and apply that focus to the task at hand, you'll be leading a more focused organization, with the capability of scaling resources up and down as you see fit.

Playing the safe game

When you outsource specific functions, you are able to reduce, minimize or distribute the risks associated with performing that particular function. For every second you spend stressing over getting it right, you could be doing something else. Instead, have confidence in knowing that your task is being managed by a complete professional, thus reducing your need to appoint any valuable brain power to that segment of your business process. I read a great story recently about one outsourcer, who outsourced his stressing and worrying. For ten minutes each day, a contractor committed to 'worry' for him, freeing him up to focus on other things. There was no need to stress - someone was looking after that already. Talk about playing it safe!

Think of the children

In this case, the 'children' are your customers. Think about their experience with your brand. Can you make their experience better with improved service, higher quality interactions, and great turnaround times? If you can do this by relieving yourself of some of the menial tasks you find yourself taking care of day in, day out, it's probably your responsibility to have someone take care of it.

Not a manager? No worries

I've heard people say things like, 'I don't know how to manage staff,' or, 'I didn't start this to have to manage people.' Guess what, you *almost* don't have to. Each of the digital platforms available out there have the functionality to help you to find, provide work to, and pay contractors, hence taking care of much of the management for you. Short of picking the contractors and giving them work, they'll do it all. After setting up milestones, your workers will make life as easy as possible for you by doing things like sending you progress reports and reporting on milestones. The platforms typically even manage your payment options for you with simplified escrow accounts and complete payment facilitation.

THE FIRST TIMER SCENARIO

While fictional, the following scenario demonstrates the approach that many outsourcers take when they launch their first outsourcing effort. This isn't designed to make the process sound simple or difficult, and by no means am I trying to intimidate you, this is simply designed to give you more clarity around the approach that many people take.

Harold comes up with a great idea for a new blog, but after some investigation, he isn't happy with the templates of the existing blogging platforms he has seen. He decides the best option for him is to get a brand new site, custom built. He proceeds to spend some time writing up content for his new site.

While assessing some of the competitive sites in his niche market with similar content, he identifies that the site requires a blog page, an 'about me' page and a 'contact' page.

Harold draws up some sketches on paper to outline what he thinks the site should look like and takes screenshots of other sites that have interesting menus, color schemes and designs.

Harold loads up Elance, his preferred outsource platform and commences writing up a brief. In this brief he documents in as much detail as possible, all aspects of the site. He lists what the purpose is, how many pages there will be, and the type of content that will be featured. He even goes into some detail, providing colors and designs he likes of existing sites, and includes the content he has drafted to date.

As part of this brief he has done his research, so he mentions he wants the website to be HTML, to not feature any 'Flash' and to be on the open Wordpress content management system. He has also already purchased his domain name and hosting package, so he adds these details.

After writing his brief, he lists an approximate price for the job, just taking a stab in the dark, he lists the price for under $500 and posts the job on Elance.

Harold is shocked to discover that within two hours he has received thirteen proposals to complete the job. A day later, there are close to thirty proposals from web developers from all over the world.

He filters through the proposals, and finds three developers that he really likes. After emailing each of them additional questions about their current workload and design choices, he gets a response from one almost instantly, stating he or she is ready to commence work.

Harold awards the job to that developer, and work commences.

Together, they have a weekly catch-up via Skype and use the built in-messenger within the Elance platform to discuss the project.

Four weeks later, the final website is finished. Harold is happy, the developer is happy, and everyone wins.

Does this sound like something that excites you? Does it sound difficult? It can be a little. Can there be complications? Sometimes. Is it worth attempting? Yes.

So you're still reading. This means you're committed, you've got your idea and you're ready to start work. Let's get on with it and talk about the nuts and bolts of online outsourcing.

QUICK TIP

Check out the project upgrades available on Freelancer.com, including 'featured project,' 'private project,' and 'sealed project,' to make your brief more compelling!

CHAPTER 2:
A HISTORY LESSON

THE HISTORY OF OUTSOURCING

The term 'freelancer' was first coined by Sir Walter Scott in 1820. The term was used to describe a mercenary warrior in medieval times, who was a 'free-lance'. This indicated that a particular lance was not sworn to any one lord, and had the flexibility to negotiate and stand in battle for multiple parties (ideally not in the same battle!). The phrase has never indicated that 'free' reflects cost of services, but more so that the agent was not tied to any one single entity.

The term was recognized as a verb (for example, "I know an engineer who freelances") by 1903 by a range of authoritative reference sources and dictionaries.

Skip forward 90 years, and in the 1990's the widespread nature of the internet opened up opportunities for global freelancing to occur; which for the first time, made logistically managing outsourced relationships simpler and more accessible for the masses.

One of the first online platforms created to deal with the opportunity the internet created was Guru.com, which was founded as eMoonlighter.com. The site was created as an online house for workers in the technology industry seeking short-term contracts.

In 1999, Elance launched the first version of their site with the view that there was an opportunity to create a platform that better supported virtual working environments.

Vworker was founded in 2001 under the name Rent A Coder. Ian Ippolito, the founder, had previously launched a website that was built to enable the sharing of source code from computer programs and launched Rent A Coder to act as a platform for intermediating paid programming projects.

Even more recently, a growing trend in crowdsourcing platforms have become increasingly evident. Platforms such as Mechanical Turk and 99 Designs enable individuals to leverage the skills and capability of multiple freelancers to complete 'micro-tasks', either in competition with other freelancers to win a contract or collaboratively as part of an overall project.

In 2005 the U.S. Department of Labor approximated that 10.3 million, or 7.4% of the US workforce were independent contractors.

Today, some of the more popular countries that freelancers occupy include; India, Indonesia, Estonia, Singapore, China, Bulgaria, Philippines, Thailand, Lithuania and Malaysia. This is due to the competitive nature of local work, education levels, the (often) low cost of living and the widespread availability of internet access.

CHAPTER 3:
VALIDATING YOUR IDEA

CONFIDENCE

An ongoing query from a number of readers has been that they are unsure of when it's the right time to outsource their first job. Prior to commencing, it is important that you're confident in yourself and the project you're working on to ensure the highest likelihood of success for the completion, delivery and longevity of your big idea.

Your personal confidence levels in the projects you're working on will significantly impact your speed to market and capability. It's fine to be simply 'testing' or 'playing' with a new idea, but when push comes to shove, those who are not confident and committed to their project will not reap the rewards associated with the execution of positively impacting the world with proactive and useful products.

Those who truly care will not only invest their own time into their project, but they'll invest their money, they'll hold themselves accountable for frequent progress and assign tight timelines with (almost) unachievable goals to accomplish. These challenges will push those who are truly confident in themselves to achieve great things.

If you are one of these people who are completely confident in yourself, your project and the capability you have for making your dent in the universe, skip to the next chapter. If you need some help to lock down what's truly important to you, continue reading.

There are a range of risks that can occur when attempting to execute on a large scale project, and without the self confidence to deliver, your uneasiness will be reflected in your communication with your contractor and your willingness to commit to your project. In many cases, those who are not confident will take less risks, will be particularly critical of their own ideas, which results in them being much slower to market, and significantly less likely to actually deliver.

In some cases, even upon completion, these entrepreneurs will sabotage or jeopardize the success of their own projects in order to reduce the fear of rejection and failure. There is a mentality and thought process going around which suggests that 'I'd rather quit and fail on my terms, rather than fail publicly'. You need not think like this, because when you're passionate and enthusiastic about what you do, failure is not an option.

While its crucial to build personal confidence in your projects, its also important to be well aware of the benefits of being critical of your own ideas. On an ongoing basis, you should be asking yourself a series of questions to ensure you're comfortable with not only your idea, but the market around you, hence instilling self confidence throughout the entire process.

These questions that you ask yourself on a frequent basis should include; is my project a good idea? What is the likelihood of this project seeing the light of day? Will my efforts be rewarded with participation from my target market? What has changed in the marketplace that will impact the success of my project?

When asking these questions, entrepreneurs are able to gauge their own sense of confidence as they continue down their development path. While being aware of market changes enables the shuffling of priorities or project requirements to best take advantage of the opportunities available.

If you've got your idea concrete and ready, but are still lacking the confidence to take action, it's important that you take a step back and identify where your limiting beliefs exist and get very clear on why it's important that your idea or product is brought to life.

This assessment needs not only take place on an entrepreneurial or aspirational level, but on a personal needs level. Do you know the direction your life is going to take? Do you know what you're aiming for? Do you know what that single point of success is and what that will mean for your life?

While not typical for a book focused on educating readers on a business related topic like outsourcing, it might worthwhile to take a trip down a side road for a moment and identify which direction you're driving in! Let's go through a quick exercise to help you identify your ideal life. When you've completed this exercise, you'll be able to make decisions about your projects with an increased confidence. This comes from knowing that you have the power to determine whether the success of your current projects will have implications that result in you living your ideal life.

THE EXERCISE

Take a moment to pull out a notepad, sketch book or your preferred word processor, and prepare to write down a series of notes. Imagine for a moment that you have more money than you could ever know what to do with. Imagine that the life you dream of today, is the one you're living, day in, day out.

Think for a moment and consider. What would my ideal life be like? What would I do? Not only 'what would I do for work, or to generate income' (remember, you don't have to generate income), but every minute of the day, what would I do? When I wake up in the morning, where do I live? Who am I waking up next to? What can I hear, is it the ocean? Is it the birds?

When I get out of bed, where do I go? Do I get breakfast? What do I eat? What do I look at while I eat? What do I do after breakfast? Who do I talk to? What do I do?

Who am I friends with? What do I do for entertainment? Do I continue to work, what am I doing?

Consider every possible aspect of your life, and list on paper 'if I could make my ideal life possible today, this is what it would consist of...'. There are no limitations. List step by step; what you see, what you feel, what you do.

Once you've completed this exercise, do some google image searches for pictures that accurately represent the ideal life you've pictured in your head and add these to a document. This is going to become your vision board, which when printed, should be attached to the walls of the areas that you occupy most.

See, when you know what you want, when you can see it, and you are passionate, excited and hungry to achieve it, you'll take huge steps in order to make it a reality. Without this vision however, you can't know what you're working towards, and without that awareness, its too easy to fall into complacency.

If you've got a passion, skill or desire to live your ideal life, and you know you've got the entrepreneurial gene to add value to the world, it's your responsibility to take action today and add this value, because when you do, you'll know just how easy it is to live your ideal life.

BUSINESS MODEL STRATEGY AND PREPARATION

When you're clear on a personal level that you know what you're striving for, the following steps are simple. Let's talk tactically about getting clear on your business or project and preparing your strategy.

Immediately understand exactly what you're looking to outsource, this could be leveraging a virtual assistant, getting a report edited or some design and development. Now take a step back and think strategy.

Consider, what are you building? What purpose will it serve? Who is your audience? Why will they care about it? If this is a business; what is your distribution method? What is your revenue model? How are you going to engage your customers?

If you've got answers to all of these questions and you can honestly commit to yourself that they are true, accurate and correct; let's get creative. It's time to add some structure to your strategy. I'd like to invite you to take a look at the business model canvas, as featured in the book 'Business Model Generation' by Alexander Osterwalder and Yves Pigneur along with 470 other co-contributors.

The business model canvas is a one page business model visualization and business design manipulation tool, which will provide you with the ultimate clarity and brainstorming potential for establishing a solid business model. Consider yourself warned, this model is for those who are prepared to no longer follow traditional conventions and embrace innovative models of value creation.

Your next step is to print the business model canvas (available for free PDF download from www.businessmodelgeneration.com) and using post-it notes fill in specific points of information in each of the 9 'building blocks'. These include customer segments, value propositions, channels, customer relationships, revenue streams, key resources, key activities, key partners and the cost structure. You'll quickly identify the value in a tool like the canvas when you've completed this task once or twice, not only does it form a powerful methodology for explaining your project to someone else, but you'll find yourself continuing to iterate on your idea to ensure the highest likelihood of success.

Perhaps the next method for building confidence occurs when you're looking to build a long term, sustainable business. We've heard time and time again that those who are successful, are so because they are capable of building strong teams around them.

Consider who you know, or who you need to meet, who will be excited about your business concept and is able to add massive value in helping you on your path. Build your personal board or advice panel, made up with mentors that you know or are able to meet. Attend local meetup groups that are based around the same topic or market that your business operates in (www.meetup.com is your friend here).

With good support, structure, milestones, goal setting and tactical strategy, you'll have the ultimate confidence as you commence your outsourcing journey.

The final method for building confidence in both yourself and your idea is in validating the business as a concept. This means you've determined what the actual problem is that you're trying to solve, your prospect customers believe that you hold the solution, and you've validated that what you're building is relevant and applicable long before any product is built. Wouldn't you rather know whether it was going to work before you invested any time and money?

This phase can't take place without actually talking to potential customers. You need to determine what their true needs are and ensure that what you're building will solve their problems. Typically, entrepreneurs build for themselves, and neglect to involve the outside world before their product is ready. My advice to you is to drop your guard and get outside the building, find your ideal customer and talk to them about the problem you're trying to solve, this will ultimately ensure that when you do launch, you'll be as close to product-market fit as possible.

CHAPTER 4:
THE PLATFORMS

THIS IS WHERE YOU'LL SPEND MOST OF YOUR TIME

The very first step is choosing which platform you want to use to outsource your work. You'll be using the same platform for everything from researching, to pitching your job, selecting a contractor, managing that contractor, and finally, paying that contractor. To help you decide, here is a comparison of some of the more popular sites. One note before you start: don't join all sites and attempt to run a profile on each simultaneously. I suspect this will result in you ending up dazed, confused and unsure about the whole experience. Pick the platform that seems to best suit you and your project and test out the experience with a small or simple job.

QUICK TIP

You should do your own research here, each platform is different and you're better off jumping into a platform that feels simple and intuitive for you.

The following evaluations of each platform are simply my own interpretations. I have not been paid by any of these companies, nor have they had any involvement in crafting the following descriptions. Only key points that I believed were of interest or differentiators are mentioned. While I has strived for accuracy, understand that anything mentioned herein could be outdated, inaccurate or incomplete; therefore, before relying on this information, visit each of the below sites (in addition to any of the many other sites) and come to your own conclusions.

ELANCE

Elance is one of the most popular websites for managing web and design outsourcing tasks. Like many of the listed sites, Elance enables you to search for contractors, post a job, select a supplier, manage the project, and pay the contractor - all within the Elance platform. In my experience, Elance contains the largest network of contractors, the quality of contractors is typically good, and scaling up your resourcing is extremely quick and easy. For example, for a recent job, I drafted a brief, selected a contractor, and had him begin work - all within forty-five minutes.

Elance operates with a 'workroom' concept, with new workrooms created for each job or projects you are running simultaneously. Here you can share messages, files, and screenshots, and all of your communications are automatically saved.

QUICK TIP

You can invite co-workers to join your Elance workroom. This creates a fantastic opportunity to work collaboratively with your freelancer and those who know your business inside and out!

With Elance, you can hire by the hour or for a complete project. Pros and cons exist for both approaches. A general rule of thumb: if you know explicitly what you want and you know exactly what goes into doing it, paying by the hour can work out fine. In many cases, however, this will generate uncertainty about how long the project may take to complete. Instead, many people prefer to to pay a set fee for a completed project. The advantage here is that any questions a contractor may have had or any changes requested by the outsourcer are typically factored in to the overarching price for the entire project (within reason).

Elance has a great escrow account model. When you agree to proceed with a new project, you can set up milestones and pre-pay your money to an escrow account. This will give the contractor the confidence in knowing that you do actually have the money, even though they won't receive it until the job is completed.

When you pay for the completed work, Elance will deduct its fee as a percentage of each payment, dependent on the project budget. The remainder is transferred directly to the contractor. There is also a small one-time account activation fee when you set up an employer account. From a hiring perspective, this is the only upfront fee you are hit with.

FREELANCER

Freelancer is an outsourcing platform that started out of Sydney, Australia. Freelancer is a popular solution for project-based tasks and incorporates a variety of options for listing your project.

Like on Elance, Freelancer features options for hiring either by the hour or for a complete project. Pros and cons exist for both approaches; you'll need to assess which model is best for you based on the project. Freelancer also provides an interesting 'contest' feature whereby an employer can post a contest with a reward and instead of following the typical model of paying a contractor and the contractor then doing the work, a number of contractors can submit an entry, from which the employer can select one and reward the fee (with an opportunity to buy multiple submissions if they wish). This is a great feature for new contractors who are looking to grow their portfolios and improve their credibility.

Freelancer has a relatively complex fee system. As an employer, it's free to join Freelancer, and posting your first project is free. There is a tiered membership plan, which reduces the applicable fees (depending on the plan selected) and each tier enables more functionality. Just assess how you plan to use the site and you'll have a pretty good idea of which tier to jump in on.

Freelancer also operates a subscription membership plan for contractors. These plans include: free, basic, standard and premium. Each of these plans require a monthly payment (outside of the free subscription) and they have scalable benefits based on the selected plan.

ODESK

oDesk is a competitive outsourcing platform which enables its users to take control of a powerful hourly rate system, and actually assess quality of work and the efficiency of workers with a range of verification features.

oDesk has a 'team room' feature which allows contractors to see each team member's activity levels, including mouse and keyboard activity. This, in conjunction with the feedback module which features a work diary and the capability of requesting webcam access or screenshots of worker's screens, ensures that the workers to whom you are paying an hourly rate are held far more accountable.

oDesk has a default percentage-based fee which it charges on top of the amount paid to the contractor.

GURU

Guru is another tool which enables the employer to simply pay for work completed.

Guru has a much higher ratio of Western contractors to emerging-country contractors. For example, the USA is home to the vast majority of workers on the platform. For this reason alone, Guru is an incredible platform for those new to outsourcing online, or those who have a project that requires verbal discussions and updates. If you would like a Western contractor specifically, this might be a good platform to try.

Guru offers a more complex fee structure than other platforms. There are a range of monthly membership subscription fees. In addition, there are percentage fees for listing a project, for utilizing the escrow account feature, and for additional payment options such as payment via cheque or wire transfer.

VWORKER

Formerly titled rentacoder.com, Vworker is a platform with a large percentage of IT roles available at the disposal of its users. Users can either pay for deliverables at completion or pay for time based on an hourly rate.

Vworker is a popular all-rounder platform for managing projects of various types and for working with contractors from a good mix of countries all over the world. As a platform, it also provides the rare feature of enabling employers to request a screenshot of their workers' screens or a shot from their webcams at any time.

With a range of options, the workers usually have a percentage deducted from their total fees as a payment to the service. There are also added benefits of using a preferred payment method.

THE COST OF DOING BUSINESS

At the end of the day, every platform differs in regard to the types of workers it engages and the tools it makes available to users. If, for example, you are looking for a tool that allows you to closely monitor the actions of your workers, you might like the screenshot or webcam request function, whereby you can ask for a status report on the spot, accompanied by a visual representation of the work done to date. In this case, oDesk or Vworker might be the right platform for you. If, alternatively, you are looking for a platform where you can post a simple job for a flat fee and get a huge range of responses, Elance may be a better option. Finally, if you have a task that would be better managed by a native English speaker, or you have a need to verbally discuss your project with your team, you might like to check out Guru.

Remember, every platform is different and each has its own benefits.

Pricing among all platforms is relatively similar, with each slightly tweaking its fee structure. A key recommendation is to consider how frequently you plan to use the service before you commit to signing up for a monthly subscription plan. This is especially the case when some of these plans can cost a significantly higher monthly fee.

Regardless of what you've read here, always do your research and review the individual terms on each platform.

PLATFORMS YOU MAY NOT HAVE CONSIDERED

Although you may not have considered it, there are a few other platforms that may be worth investigating, these are not necessarily conventional outsourcing platforms, however they can certainly be used to simplify or reduce output required for specific jobs.

TASK RABBIT

Task Rabbit is a relatively new, US only service, which has taken an interesting approach to enabling the outsourcing of physical tasks. Like any platform, contractors bid on jobs, and once selected, will complete the task.

The difference here is that these tasks are typically 'real world', meaning that Task Rabbit is often used for assistance in tasks such as assembling Ikea furniture, delivering a product or helping you to move house. While I don't talk too much about physical outsourcing in this book, Task Rabbit is worth mentioning. I had a great experience using it in a corporate setting when I needed to have someone next to me doing some specific data entry work and the service was near flawless.

FANCY HANDS

Fancy Hands is another relatively new service with a twist. All Fancy Hands contractors are US based and highly skilled to take on administrative tasks. Rather than bid on jobs, the outsourcer will list the job they want completed, a contractor will step in, determine how complex the job is, and complete it accordingly. Fancy Hands is a subscription only service, so prior to allocating work, users must make a call on how much they plan to use the service, and pay for this accordingly on a monthly basis.

FIVERR

Fiverr is possibly one of the most simplistic and underrated sites on the internet. Users post what they're willing to do for $5, and anyone can take them up on that. Everything from logo design to internet marketing advice; it isn't traditional outsourcing, but I bet you'll be amazed at what you can get done.

CHAPTER 5:
VIRTUAL ASSISTANTS

It doesn't matter whether you're a high-rolling five time entrepreneur, or a first timer with an interesting idea, we all get overloaded with work to do. In many cases, it's common to employ support staff very early in the start-up phase to ensure administrative (or tedious) tasks are completed and don't slip through the cracks.

In the last five years, it has become increasingly common to engage support or administrative staff via digital outsourcing platforms to assist in day to day work. In essence, a virtual assistant (VA) works in much the same way that a local employee would operate. As an employer, your role is to communicate tasks (typically of an administrative nature) which require completing in as fast and as high a quality as possible.

Virtual assistants often operate within a corporate or agency type environment and are engaged and managed through a bigger organization. They will often also bid for direct administrative rolls via platforms like Elance. An additional benefit is as a result of the typical engagement and payment structure, in many cases virtual assistants can either operate via a subscription package to provide support on an ongoing basis, or work on a month to month or week to week time frame, on a retainer of a specific number of hours for that set period.

There are a range of additional benefits that can occur when engaging a virtual assistant. Firstly, by leveraging an international virtual assistant, you will only be paying for the hours actually worked, and you can focus on saving 60% to 70% of local staffing costs, due to you not having a staff member occupying a desk regardless of workload. Like all outsourcing, you can also take advantage and leverage around the clock operations due to your employee functioning in a different timezone to you. Everyone loves to work (and make money) while they sleep.

Work that is typically engaged by a virtual assistant may include: writing, formatting important documents, diary management, web based research, travel bookings, data entry or even CRM support. However, the best virtual assistants are not limited to these tasks, some are highly skilled and can take on a range of more complex jobs, these could include: liaising with clients and customers, telephone support (reception assistance or technical support), lead generation and opportunity identification, media monitoring, event management or digital marketing.

If you are in the market to engage a virtual assistant, it pays to do your research. There are literally hundreds of platforms and agencies that manage this process. You should always request a short trial phase to determine how a particular company's virtual assistant facilitation process operates, in terms of management, accounts/payment, skill and capability, and human resources. Next time you have a menial administrative function that you're working through, why no try out leveraging a freelancer and assess your progress!

HOW MUCH DOES MY VA KNOW ABOUT ME?

Perhaps the most frequent query I receive when people are considering engaging a virtual assistant is based around the security of their personal data. A long standing relationship with a good virtual assistant will result in them likely knowing everything about you, from credit card details, to family history, to the make of car you drive, your address, even your medical history. This is often a tough pill to swallow, however there are a number of small tactics you can implement to ensure your identity (and bank account) remains safe.

Firstly, when selecting a virtual assistant, you should always be on the mission to find one with a solid history, with good ratings and references. There is absolutely nothing wrong with asking a potential hire for former managerial references so that you can conduct a check. By doing this simple task, you will greatly reduce the potential risk of having a bad experience.

After you've hired your virtual assistant, a smart tactic is to create new user accounts (with new passwords) for the websites you would like your contractor to access on your behalf. This is especially important if you like to use the same password for all of your web services.

One final idea is around the security of credit cards. Ideally, you'd provide your credit card details to your virtual assistant so that they're empowered to make specific purchases on your behalf (obviously with agreed limits in place), however rather than giving a new contractor your existing credit card details, inquire with your bank about preloaded credit cards. Many banks provide cards where you can add (let's say) $500 in credit to the card, with a maximum daily spend of $100. As expenses are made, you can be notified via email, and if something appears to be fraudulent, you can have the card cancelled.

This is a great way to both empower your assistant to work autonomously while protecting your most important assets.

CHAPTER 6:
GETTING YOUR REQUIREMENTS DOWN

KNOWING WHAT YOU WANT

So you've got a fantastic idea for a new website. In fact, for the purposes of this chapter, let's assume you want to create a new website for yourself or your business. The same principles, of course, can be applied to any situation, simply apply a little common sense.

You've done all of the research, there is a customer need, your partners are waiting, and you've got marketing tactics ready to roll. It's time to get to work.

You can't simply jump onto an outsourcing platform and write up a brief stating, 'I need a new website for my business.' Consider firstly the purpose and format of the website. Does it need an online store, a newsletter signup, a contact form, social media integration, an 'about' page, a product portfolio, a blog or news section, or even a membership login section? What do you want to be on the home page? What other pages do you need and in what order should they appear in the menu? Do you even have a menu?

If you're unable to answer 'yes' or 'no' to any of these questions, you've got work to do.

Think about the structure and divide each page of the site into modules. What modules do you want? Where do you want these modules to feature? What color scheme do you want for the website? Do you have a logo? Where should it appear? Start by drawing these on paper, this will go a long way in helping you to determine what the users experience will be like.

Consider usability in this process. Do some research into trends in your industry. How are your competitors quoting for a product or pushing their social media pages? Learn from them and include all of these observations in your brief.

THE EXAMPLE

Are you feeling overwhelmed? Don't, because there is a simple way of doing this. Firstly, list the key features of your proposed site, then take a few sheets of paper and draw your site. Draw where the main menu, the header, and your logo should sit, then draw in your content sections, even considering what colors should appear where.

The following highlights an example demonstrating some of the points you should consider including in your requirements.

Content Section A:

Home page:

- Include text included in this section.
- Attach images that will feature in this section.
- Include any links, forms or buttons that should appear in this section.

Contact page:

- Include contact form, containing areas full name, email address and comment box.
- Note that on completion of the form, data should be sent to info@mydomain.com.
- Include text appearing prior to contact form and text after contact form.

Product list:

- List each product by category (product images, descriptions and any other details should be included at this time).
- List these in a grid formation with four products along the top line, and four rows. At the end of each row, provide arrows to link to the next page.
- Include links to 'more information' about each product, large product images, and the Add To Cart feature under each product."

Of course you need to provide a significantly more comprehensive document to your contractor, but this gives you an indication of one method for articulating 'what' content should appear 'where'.

Legends, as mentioned above, can be very helpful. You might, for example, mark different modules on drawings, demonstrating the desired color scheme for that section (for example, link color: blue, rollover link color: red, background color: light grey, header text: blue). Support these color guidelines with screenshots from other websites with similar or the same colors you are looking for. If you have a brand style guide, this should be provided to your contractor in the very early stages, as it will very clearly impact the design of the website (and simplify the early stages of the project). If you don't have an operational style guide (which is more often the case for entrepreneurs or small business owners), you should be seeking out a designer whose past work you like, because his or her eye for design will become increasingly important throughout the project.

When you're considering what you want your website to look like and what content should appear within it (let's assume you've got a pretty good understanding of what your competitors are doing), you should start to take screenshots of other websites you like and include these in a word document, accompanied by notes and links to the relevant page. These screenshots and links will be extremely useful for your designer.

If you like a particular type of blog format, the way a vertical page slider looks, or the way two color gradients integrate, take shots of all of these points. Any good designer will be able to apply the aspects you like from other sites into your website using your own colors and styles. If you are flexible, it will also pay to take screenshots of and provide links to your competitors' pages, as your designer may well come up with a new or different way or displaying similar content.

The biggest takeaway from this section is that you need to know what you want. Know what you want your website to look like, what you want it to do, the pages that will feature within it, and have all of the content ready to go.

At this point, you should document your requirements. Your requirements document should feature all of the above mentioned detail about your desired website so that the instant you select a contractor, he or she can read up and get working. With good requirements and content ready, your contractor will be able to reduce time asking questions and waiting on you.

When you write up your requirements, remember you're articulating what you want your website to do. If you skip on the detail here, you can expect a low-quality product. Add as much detail as possible and ensure that your contractor knows exactly what you're looking for.

For the purposes of this section, some key aspects you might consider including in a requirements document include:

1. Break up the website by pages, as previously discussed. Have sections for the home page, blog, news, contact, about, portfolio, products, and any other pages you might have.

2. Draw on a series of A4 sheets of paper the basic website layout for each page and, using a legend, break the site into sections, for example 'Content

Section A.' You'll be able to then reference each section in any accompanying notes.

3.   Ensure you've articulated what content should appear on every page. For example, "the main menu, header, and logo will remain consistent on each page. When you roll over the menu items, the individual items should flash sliver like they do at www.inspirationsite.com. When you click on the header, which will state "Header Text" in Arial font and should be larger than 32pt font, it should link to the homepage of the site, regardless of which page the user is on. Social links should appear below 'Content Section A' at the bottom right of the page, and there should be a Facebook 'like' button just below the bottom right corner of the page, which links to www.facebook.com/mycompanypage."

4.   As you articulate the functions of every page, you should include the color scheme of the website. If you have brand guidelines or any brand requirements, these should be provided. If not, and you are flexible as to how the site is designed, provide any other material you might have that are on brand, for example, brochures, sales letters, email signatures or even business cards.

5.   Find inspirational elements on other sites that you love. If you like the way a particular website element looks or functions, take a screenshot and provide this image with a link to the page and a note to describe what you like about it and how you would like it to be implemented. This will give your designer clarity around your design expectations.

6.   If you're looking at building a collaborative relationship with your contractor, also take screenshots of key features on your competitors' websites in order to collaborate on how you might be able to do it better.

7.   Have the content ready. This is key. So many sites are held up and not delivered on time because the outsourcer only has positional content for the purposes of development and has not confirmed content that is ready to go. When you engage a contractor, you'll be excited to get the new site ready as quickly as possible. While this is great, you should always ensure that they have all of the content they need to design the site around the content and not require that you change the content and your message because you need to fit it into a freshly-built template.

8.   Ensure you describe the 'what' and 'how.' If you're referencing links or buttons, be clear about what these should do and where they should go. If you want the website to have a feature, ensure the developer knows what that feature is and what it should do.

The key thing to remember when writing up your requirements is to make them simple. Leave nothing to chance. You should be able to give it to someone who isn't technically savvy and have him or her understand and be able to explain the website to you, highlighting everything from purpose to design to usability. If he or she is able to do this, you've probably written a cohesive requirements document.

TECHNICALITIES AND
CONTENT MANAGEMENT SYSTEMS

Although we don't want to dive too deep into this topic, I thought it might be useful to cover this briefly. In the case of any web development job, you'll typically use a content management system (CMS). The CMS is the back-end infrastructure that allows you, as an administrator, to log into your website and change any part of the site you like, typically content, but in theory, everything from design to content to functionality without any programming skills at all.

Many web developers will prefer one of a couple of content management systems over others. In most cases, this isn't a big issue, but here's a key tip: if you've never managed a website before, stick to one of the more popular solutions such as Wordpress, Drupal, or Joomla!

QUICK TIP

Open source can be great, as you'll have the added benefit of third party developers working to improve that CMS's operating environment. For a great list of what's available check out this great Wikipedia page:
http://en.wikipedia.org/wiki/
List_of_content_management_systems

Another important technical aspect that any outsourcer should learn about is web standards. You should have a basic understanding about the programming languages required to build your desired website.

Ten years ago, it was amazing to include Flash elements in your website to enhance the interactivity of a website, but since 2007 and the introduction by Apple of the iPhone, there has been a strong push against Flash as a development tool for a range of reasons.

Depending on the nature of your product, you should understand the types of programming languages required. Based on the development feature set and approach, understand why you would choose one over the other.

BROWSER COMPATIBILITY

That's right, browser compatibility. Not a sexy or fun topic to talk about, but fairly simple and very important. When writing up your technical requirements for your website, clearly define that you want your website to be experienced in a similar way from browser to browser. In fact, I'd suggest you request that your website functions with at most, a 99% variance between the recent versions of the most-used browsers, specifically Microsoft Internet Explorer, Apple Safari, Mozilla Firefox, Google Chrome and Opera.

You should also understand that if you are looking for a modern website and are looking to use modern web standards, you'll have to draw a line as to where your website will not necessarily be supported. For example, if someone boots up a late 1990's Dell, loads up a prehistoric version of Microsoft's Internet Explorer, and goes to your new website, you should be aware that it's not necessarily going to load up your world-class design.

It's the nature of the beast for new websites to be built to the most recent design standards, provided your new product isn't specifically geared to a market who notoriously refuse to upgrade their system. Generally speaking, if you build your website to recent standards, you'll be happy with the result. If you are particularly concerned with specific code, you can actually have a notification pushed to users of unsupported browsers stating that your website is best displayed with a more recent browser, with steps to upgrade their current system.

Be aware of what is currently available and discuss this with the contractor you choose. This isn't a difficult point to understand, but it's important that you're aware of it and discuss this as you communicate your expectations.

REALITY

The examples in this book are strongly focused on customized web design and development projects, however, the reality is that I actually don't think you need a custom build. I bet you think you do, but reality is that you don't.

I have a go-to tactic for all new websites that I build. Here is my workflow for just about any website:

1. I visit www.bluehost.com (or comparable domain name and hosting provider), purchase domain name and hosting, typically for under $100.

2. I head to www.themeforest.net and or www.woothemes.com, and I'll search for a 'Wordpress' theme that reflects my site and brand, and purchase it for around $60.

3. I log into the hosting package at www.bluehost.com and configure a Wordpress installation (there is plenty of information on how to do this online, simply google "how to install wordpress on bluehost").

4. I log into Wordpress, upload the theme, and start editing content.

5.   If I need changes made, I'll contact a developer via an outsourcing platform, pay them for 2 hours of their time to tweak the code to make changes to structure, colors and design.

This workflow requires zero development skill, and you'll walk away in half an hour with a brand new, incredibly professional website.

CHAPTER 7:
WRITING THE BRIEF

WHAT'S THE BRIEF

Your brief is essentially the job board posting. This is the title and description you'll provide to get contractors interested in the opportunity and bidding on the job accordingly. The goal here is to provide a clear and concise description of the task at hand so that any number of contractors are clear on exactly what is required.

You should also keep in mind that the goal is to generate as many bids for the job as possible, as a result, you need to consider SEO (Search Engine Optimization) in your brief. A virtual assistant, is no doubt searching for opportunities that reference the phrase 'virtual assistant' in the title, so in order to make sure your jobs are found by the most appropriate contractors, list keywords in the article and description that you believe your ideal contractor is searching for.

Your brief should feature short sentences, have one possible interpretation and be suitable for a 2nd grade reading level. You want your contractor to truly understand the task at hand, and if you're using buzz words or short hand, it's quite possible that you'll end up selecting a provider that isn't as compatible with you as you'd like.

BUT WHAT DO I SAY?

The brief should generally be quite simple to write. Just consider what you would need to tell someone so that they can (stick with me here) draw your website on a piece of paper. Your brief really should just be as simple as just a few paragraphs to help you track down a few key contractors to choose from.

This is my preferred methodology for writing a brief:

1. What:

Introduce yourself and explain what you do, what your project is, and what the desired effect is of having the work completed.

2. Detailed 'what':

Break down in some depth what you're actually looking for. An example would be:

"This a 5-page website to promote a new product. The home page will feature text and images; the product page will feature large screenshots with text and embedded YouTube videos; the blog will be a standard blog (I should be able to edit this via the selected CMS in the deliverables section); the pricing page will be a pricing chart with 5 different payment options, which should integrate with a standard checkout package or plugin; finally, the contact page will feature a web form that will e-mail to me, an address with Google map integration, and a phone number."

3. Deliverables:

List exactly what you expect to actually 'get' as a result of the completed work. In the case of a website, you might ask for:

- All designs for each page of the website in the relevant layered files (this will typically be an Adobe Photoshop, Illustrator or Fireworks file).
- The website in its entirety, developed and available for access using your domain name, and on your hosting package.

4. Look and feel:

How deeply and well-formulated your current brand strategy is will dictate how much clarity you're able to provide here. If you have a current website, logo, desired colors (right down to HEX/RGB codes), fonts, and design principals then these should all be provided in the brief. It should be communicated that these colors, fonts and design principals should all be be strictly utilized.

If you don't have a detailed brand strategy, this is a great opportunity to create one using new design assets that complement your company.

5. Layout:

Put some thought into the design and layout of your site. Do you have any thoughts about whether you want a vertical or horizontal menu? Do you know where you want your logo to sit? If you do, make this known now. If not, search around at others' sites and use these to brainstorm what it is that you'd like or dislike for your own site. If you don't know, or particularly care, and are looking for some guidance from your designer, make it known in your brief that you want to work with a designer in a collaborative environment all the way through the design process.

6. Extra resources:

Provide links to aspects of other websites you like, either entirely or screenshots of parts of websites, for example: menus, scrolling bars, and contact forms. Send links to your competitors' pages in order for the contractor to get an idea of how they are positioned in the market.

BRIEF VERSUS REQUIREMENTS

So you've decided you want a website, you've written a great brief, and you've drafted your website requirements (from the previous chapter). It's now time to get this thing online and get some bids coming in!

You have two options. Firstly, you can provide your brief in as simple a way as possible. Without going into elaborate depth, simply describe:

- What your website (or project) will be built to achieve.
- How many pages there are going to be, highlighting basic functionality and design.

This strategy will get you the highest number of bids because of the high-level detail. As a result, you'll be able to review a huge list of prospect contractors and zoom in on one or short-list a couple accordingly.

There is a second strategy that slightly differs, however this isn't one that I'd recommend if you're concerned about confidentiality, intellectual property or your competitors finding out information about your new project. This strategy requires that you provide a significant amount of information upfront in your brief (including your full requirements document), so there is no ambiguity about what you actually want. This strategy should net you better-qualified bids. You are likely to get a much shorter list of proposals, which should reduce the amount of time you spend validating the bidders. If you'd prefer this option, write a short brief outlining what the project is, then attach the detailed functional requirements.

Regardless of the strategy you choose, before you select a contractor, my recommendation is that you provide (at the very least), the short-listed bidders with your full requirements. This enables you to select a few that look like strong bidders and enable them to update their bid (or withdraw it) when they know what you're looking for in great depth.

THE EXPECTATIONS OF YOU

Unless you clearly specify it in the brief, (in the case of a website) you'll typically need to purchase the website domain name and hosting package separately to the project. You'll want to provide these details to your contractor as soon as practical to ensure he or she can configure your content management system and get this loaded on your hosting platform. There are a huge range of contractors available to help you complete these tasks so if you find yourself stuck, just ask. Check out the resources section near the end of this book for more information.

THE BRIEF - FEATURED OR FREE

Many of the outsourcing platforms enable you to pay to have your brief featured above others. In most cases, I would suggest that you don't need to pay extra to make your brief stand out. Consider this to be similar to the SEO (Search Engine Optimization) versus SEM (Search Engine Marketing) decision. You can choose to write a little and pay to have it featured more prominently, or you can invest some more time, add some more detail (and in turn, more keywords) and appear in search results organically.

If you have a detailed brief, it will typically appear well in searches on your selected outsourcing platform. As a result, you probably won't need to pay the extra few bucks to have your brief 'featured.'

For the majority of jobs, there are thousands of capable and honest contractors on each of these sites. If you post a well-thought-out and detailed brief, with a reasonable pricing bracket, you'll be satisfied with the interest you receive in the first few hours, regardless of whether you go featured or free.

The only reason I'd suggest you should 'feature' a brief would be in the case that it is particularly urgent that you kick off the project. But in any case (even if listing it as a free job), you're likely to have a sufficient number of proposals in the first 24 hours (dependent on the job, brief and price listed).

CHAPTER 8:
PRICING YOUR PROJECT

Prior to posting your job, you'll be positioned with what might be an awkward predicament. You'll typically be asked whether you want to pay via an hourly rate or with a total project fee. If this is your first time, it's important to know that there are a range of methods that exist for determining an appropriate cost for your project. Below we will examine a few unique methods. In this process, there are a few key principals:

1.   Do your research. Look at what others are charging or paying on your outsourcing platform of choice. This is easy to browse, and you'll be far better informed about what to expect and what's reasonable.

2.   Don't always look for the cheapest price. You're already saving huge amounts of money by outsourcing online. Take the time to choose a contractor you believe you can build a relationship with, rather than the one with the lowest bid.

3.   If it sounds too good to be true, it probably is. No one is going to work forever, especially for a one-off fixed price. Understand that while you'll be offered things like 'unlimited revisions,' this is within reason. You'll need to reinvest after a point if you find there is a continual back-and-forth.

One favorite strategy for picking your price is to go down the road or pick up the phone and speak with a local designer, developer or contractor. Explain your project and ask him or her for a quote for development. This will give you a good base price to compare with.

For one of my projects, I'd worked out that for a basic website I could expect to pay around 10% to an outsourced contractor of what I'd pay by walking into a local design agency. In this case, the local agency had expected the job would cost around $1,500, whereas by outsourcing, I was able to get the entire job completed for just under $200. If you are building something more complex, like a mobile application or software tool, you can often expect to pay between 5% and 8% for an outsourced contractor, as you'll find your local agency may well not be skilled enough to take on the task and will need to bring on staff or even outsource themselves (although they likely won't tell you that) to complete the job.

Once you've got an idea of a broad price that sounds 'about right' based on your project, the platform, and the contractors bidding on your brief, one strategy is to select a bidder with a moderately high bid. Sounds counterproductive? Read on.

If, for example, you are building a website and expect design and development work for the full project should cost around $200, you might go on Elance and select the price bracket, inviting bids up to $500. You'll likely get up to 30 bids, depending on the quality of your brief, with a majority ranging between $100 and $200. As you filter through the bids, focus on those that sit in the $200 to $300 bracket as these contractors are more likely to have read the brief and tailored a specific reply to you, rather than a copy and paste job, which is often submitted by so many others.

While going through this process, answer any questions that prospect contractors might ask, as this also demonstrates they've paid particular attention to your drafted requirements and are responding accordingly.

IS PREPAYING SCARY?

One of the most frightening experiences a new outsourcer can encounter occurs when you've just selected a contractor for your exciting new project, and he or she asks for 50% up front. This often isn't a significant amount of money, but many contractors will request this to prevent themselves from being taken advantage of.

Remember, it's a two-way street. Most Westerners go into outsourcing with a lack of trust or confidence in the loyalty, capability and ethics of the contractors they are considering engaging. While it's fair to be wary and to take the necessary precautions to ensure you have a good experience, you should remember that it's quite likely that your job may well be the sole source of revenue for your contractor for the following weeks. As a result, he or she is going to (rightly so) take precautions to ensure that as an employer, you have the funds available to pay when required.

As a result, there are a couple of key points to consider. It's entirely possible that your contractors will inform you that they have one key model for payments. This could be; 50% upfront, 50% at completion; 20% up front and the remainder to be paid at milestones throughout the project; or any other variation.

When outsourcing web design work, the maximum amount I'd suggest you provide as an upfront payment is 50%. Do this only if you are completely confident in the capability of the contractor and want that contractor, specifically, to complete the work (based on his or her portfolio, clients, quality of work, and any other varying factors).

If the concept of prepaying frightens you, many of the outsourcing platforms offer an escrow service. This means you pay the money at the start of the job to an account managed by the platform, and both parties (you and your contractor) can see the funds are there. When you're comfortable that the work has been delivered you can either release the total amount or release it in block payments at key project milestones.

Using the escrow program and loading it with funds early will instill in your contractor confidence that you have the money and you're willing to part with it. If the contractor sees it there, he or she is more likely to deliver a quick product in order to receive a quick payment.

MY BASIC PAY SCALES

It actually doesn't make a lot of sense to write out 'typical' pay scales, as these vary greatly, depending on what is actually requested and delivered. Regardless, many people have asked for indicative rough figures that I'd expect to pay, so here they are.

Web design

When outsourcing design (note: not development, only design), it's typical to request complete delivery of image files only (often in PSD (Photoshop) format). If you have a website developer ready to put the pieces together, or want specific design expertise, this can be a fantastic way of building the design foundations of your project. You might expect to spend between $100 and $200 for up to three pages, with fairly simple design and minimal artistic creation.

Web design and development

When outsourcing customized web design and development, you would typically approach a freelancer with the intent that they will go through the two step process of providing designs for approval, followed by the complete technical development phase of the website. The typical delivery for this type of project would be the request that upon completion, the site is delivered, deployed and 'live' on your hosting package. In this case, you could expect typical cost for a simple, clean (up to ten page) website to be between $200 and $500 subject to the complexity of the development phase. In this case, you are best having all of the website content completed prior to engaging a freelancers.

Website template configuration

As earlier mentioned, if you have purchased your domain name, hosting, and an applicable theme for your desired content management system, you can provide all of these details to a contractor and request that they do the technical work in setting up the final site for you. This will generally take a few hours, and will generally cost less than $50, resulting in the full website going live for under $200 and being complete in a day. It's hard to beat that!

Copywriting

For the purposes of this example it is assumed that you might be looking for 3 articles about your chosen niche at around 300 words each to be distributed on a corporate blog. You can typically expect to spend less than $20 - $30 per article, however this varies greatly based on skill level of the contractor. You should also remember that ideally you will be looking for someone here who writes with a strong command of the English language.

Proofreading

Proofreading can typically be based on a per-1000-words rate. Remember, you're looking for someone here who is ideally fluent in English. For a highly skilled contractor, you could expect to spend close to $60 for 1000 words, however with economies of scale, there is room to negotiate if you are working to a much larger word count.

Mobile application development

Mobile application quoting is always a complex process because there is a huge number of variables at play. As an example, imagine you want to build a native iOS (iPhone) application that has a few screens and is relatively simple with regards to data flow. In this case, you may expect to pay between $1,000 and $3,000, but this is very much based on the work being completed. Note: mobile developers are extremely sought after at present, and as a result, similar work could be valued in excess of $15,000, with the possibility of increasing to around $30,000 or significantly more at a local development agency.

As mentioned, these figures and scenarios are only rough indications. Remember, the more information and clarity you have around your project, the simpler this process will be for you. If your brief is simple and transparent, you'll immediately have a pretty good indication of the appropriate price based your contractor's bids.

Another option to encourage as many bids as possible is to select price brackets rather than a specific price (for example, '$0 - $500' rather than '$260'). Price brackets will create an environment where the bidders are able to assess your brief and provide their bids based on what you're requesting from them. If you don't price via this bracket method, you'll find that the bidding will become increasingly competitive (which isn't necessarily a bad thing), and you'll encourage low cost (possibly low quality) contractors to bid who will undercut your quoting price and their competitors in the hope they get through.

These are all very much general circumstances and any number of situations could arise when you create your brief, but in my experience it's hard to go wrong when providing a clear brief with a broad price bracket. This will encourage the most bids and give you a solid playing field from which to select your dream team.

QUICK TIP

Providing a specific price encourages multiple bidders to
make their bids for the same amount. In reality, one of the
more popular strategies is to encourage bidders to provide
a bid unique to your project as the result of considering
your brief in depth. When this occurs, you can select a
bidder who may not necessarily be the cheapest but will
provide the most value.

CHAPTER 9:
PULLING THE TRIGGER

You've written up your pitch and requirements. Now for the exciting part! It's time to choose a contractor. There are many methods for choosing from the bids you receive on your new job, and the single biggest mistake you can make is choosing a contractor based exclusively on price. Another mistake is spending too much time analyzing bids. Research is always your friend, and taking a deep look into each of your bidders is great, but once you get to a point of having filtered down the selection to two bidders from a pool of ten or more, choosing either one of them will generally be fine. Remember, analysis paralysis.

One potential differentiator is in the quality of the bid. Though many contractors will attach a range of images demonstrating their quality of work, which is always a nice touch, never rely solely on this. Dive deeper and look at their portfolio and past work ratings on the platform.

Though this may be difficult, try to avoid judging the quality of a contractor based purely on their written English skills in the bid. Many of these contractors will know English as a second language (or third, or forth), and the key point to remember is that as long as they know enough to understand your requirements and are able to collaborate with you, you'll be able to get through the project. More than anything, be able to look past the bid and assess the contractors based on their capability.

Be careful of contractors or contracting organizations with a huge number of 5 star reviews. While they may just be amazing, I always like to see one or two 3 or 4 star reviews, as this demonstrates a bit of authenticity. It's very easy to go and register an account and award yourself a job, pay yourself and give yourself a 5 star review. As a result, you really want to dive down and do your research, always be careful choosing the cheapest bid, while each of the outsourcing platforms (for example, Elance) do a great job of monitoring for sketchy behavior from contractors, if it looks too good to be true, it probably is and it pays to be vigilant.

As has already been mentioned, many people choose to outsource because of the huge low-cost benefits. Don't get too caught up on this. Every contractor you look at will be relatively well-priced (comparatively) and you'll quickly identify that it is very hard to compare purely on price given the volume of bids that are very comparable. If you've short-listed a couple of ideal contractors based on capability and portfolio, then look at price as a secondary indicator. When I have five ideal contractors with varying price points, I'll rarely choose the cheapest from a price perspective, I'll typically be looking for someone down the middle of the list, with the possibility of going up to the higher end.

To summarize, always remember to do your research, assess the bid, and look at ratings and portfolios on the platform you're working on. In a contractors portfolios you'll probably see a range of jobs completed for clients; take the time to go onto the client sites and evaluate the quality of the work.

If you're still unsure, you can always actually contact past customers via their websites and ask them about their experiences with the contractor. This is a surefire way of learning exactly how the contractor worked, as you'll get an unbiased view directly from the past customer. To better manage the risk, this is a great strategy to identify whether the contractor is looking to scam you or not. It would be very easy for a scammer to take screenshots of 50 well-designed websites and add them to his or her portfolio, so reaching out to the actual website owners, verifying that the contractor did actually build this site, and asking about the experience isn't a bad move.

Remember, these techniques are not foolproof. You need to apply common sense and choose a contractor that works for you.

CHAPTER 10:
MANAGING THE PROJECT

Managing the ongoing project is one of the more difficult aspects of outsourcing. The most important part is ongoing communication by communicating as much as possible throughout the entire process to ensure your contractor is on the right path.

PROJECT MANAGEMENT

The most crucial stage of any project is in the initial delegation of tasks, this is where the contractor can leave with a clear understanding of what needs to take place, or no idea whatsoever. Firstly, you should clearly communicate with your contractor that they do not have a license to waste time, don't set tasks like "research X, and see how you go", this says to them "I don't know how long this should take, have a search around." I've heard horror stories where contractors have spent days researching for a task that could have taken 20 minutes. The trick here is to break up tasks, prioritize them accordingly, and set an hour cap for each. Start with a simple, short, repetitive task to build both your confidence and theirs, then follow this with short tasks.

Another trick is to have your contractor rephrase the task back to you after you've issued it to them. This can happen either in a typed message or verbally, but you'll quickly identify whether they have understood the task at hand.

Like with managing any project, a key function is to set up timelines with intended outcomes and very closely monitor progress. By going through that initial project management phase, you'll ensure that both you and your contractor understand all of the required outcomes associated with the project.

When considering the milestone setup phase, for the best result, you should communicate your desired delivered outcomes, along with dates, and give your contractor a chance to provide their feedback, this will enable them to communicate outcomes from the very beginning of the project and they'll be aware of the bigger picture. Some outsourcing platforms enable you to build these milestones into the project requirements, whereas others will simply require you manage this via the built-in conversational tools.

For a basic web design job, your milestones might be: Start, approval of design, front-end development completion, integration with CMS completion, final changes, and final delivery. This means that throughout the project, you're maintaining close contact with your contractor and you'll be able to identify when a project might be being derailed early enough to scale up the communication to resolve any issues that may occur.

REPORTING

Another great move is to set up regular reports or meetings. For a long-term project, you might, at the very least, request a written report to be provided on a weekly basis. If you're very engaged or working with a particularly complex project, use these reports in conjunction with a weekly catch-up via Skype or an alternative video calling platform. You'll get the best result when you can see each other and talk through what's working and what still requires thought. This is also great for collaboration early in the project.

I'd encourage you to establish a written reporting template that the contractor provides to you daily, weekly or at any other duration that makes sense given the project timeline. You should be able to communicate with them what they need to keep track of, how frequently they should be in touch with you and what constitutes an emergency. The idea here is to reduce your administrative burden, not increase it due to constant contact. The trick is to know how much authority you're willing to delegate to your contractor, and empower them to make basic decisions and report on these accordingly in order to keep the project moving.

In a past website development project that I managed, one of my contractors simply went quiet for two weeks. He mentioned on a number of occasions that he had been sick, which was fine from my perspective, but outlining the importance of weekly meetings or reports may well have set the expectation of regular action taking place.

One huge mistake people make when outsourcing is changing or tweaking the project too much throughout the process. It's fine to have new ideas and thoughts on new design or functionality throughout the process, but when you do so, best practice states that you should immediately document exactly (in detail) what should change and how it should change, as well as booking a meeting to discuss the changes and how they might impact other aspects of the project, costs or timelines.

If you don't hear from your contractor for a few days, or you're not happy with the delivery provided throughout the process, it's important to take action immediately. Schedule a meeting and get the project back on track, or you'll continue on a downward spiral.

CHAPTER 11:
CLOSE TO COMPLETION

FINALLY HAPPY?

Are you happy with where your project has ended up? That is, are you really happy? In many cases, you'll get access to unlimited revisions from your contractor, but often the terms state that this is up until the point of final delivery. So before you accept the final project, make sure you've ironed out the creases and you're happy to launch.

MANAGING THE DELIVERY

If you've built a website (once again, as an example), it's quite possible that the contractor has built this on his or her own server and has shared an obscure link with you in order for you to view the progress of the project to date.

Your contractor will likely have configured your CMS (Content Management System) environment, so the first step will be requesting any relevant links or login details for the back-end of the website. Alternatively, many of the content management systems on the market have an option to create additional licenses or login credentials, so if your project was to update an existing site, you might well have created a 'contractor' login account to your CMS, which means you'll already have complete access.

You'll also need to purchase (if you haven't already) your domain name and website hosting package. There are thousands of companies that sell domains and hosting and almost all are very competitive. Your best bet here is to shop around, review the different hosting options, and select appropriately. Given the amount of competition in this space, you shouldn't be persuaded to spend a significant amount of money on this. As a general rule, don't pay more than $100 for a domain name and an entry-level hosting package per year. Don't get caught up in purchasing too many additional add-ons when purchasing your hosting - many companies will offer advanced SEO packages or a website builder tool. If these sound of interest to you, try them out; however, many of these are not necessary and are simply a last-minute grab for cash from the respective domain or hosting company.

Before you buy, understand that your domain name is the address a visitor will type to get to your site, for example, www.mattkellydomainname.com. Think of website hosting as the block of land you purchase on which to build your house. Without the block of land, there is nowhere to put the house. Without your hosting package, there isn't anywhere to store your website.

While you're looking at hosting packages, you might consider whether you'd like to get an email address (or multiple) for your new domain name. For example, I might want matt@mattkellydomainname.com and sales@mattkellydomainname.com. If this is the case, ensure your hosting package includes an allowance for multiple email addresses. Many entry-level packages will include 1 to 5 email addresses by default.

When purchasing your hosting, ensure that the hosting package is capable of integrating with your content management system of choice. In some rare cases, the 'starter' hosting package will require you utilize a proprietary website development tool. If in doubt, call up the company and ask which of its hosting packages best integrates with Wordpress (or your chosen CMS). If you have a bad customer service experience with this process, move on. There is plenty of competition in the domain name and web hosting space!

When you've bought your domain name and hosting package, the best thing to do is forward your confirmation emails (ensuring there are no personal details contained) from the hosting company directly to your developer and suggest that he or she uploads your new website to this package.

QUICK TIP

An alternative option for email hosting (given many hosting companies charge an added fee for email addresses, and often have horrible user interface), is to create a Google Apps account (these start at around $60 each year). For an entry level website, you can create your Google Apps account, add a small piece of tracking code to your website (your developer can help you with this), and configure your new email addresses in the Google Apps management tool.

The advantage here is that Google provides the entry-level package for a relatively low cost for a limited number of addresses, enabling you to manage your email through the Gmail interface, which many argue is one of the best. Understand that this will not be an @gmail.com address, but they will be @yourdomain.com addresses, so from your customers perspective, there will be no difference here.

LEAVING FEEDBACK

Feedback is essentially currency on many of these outsourcing sites, as having good feedback is akin to having a list of referrals for future jobs. Remember when you were reviewing all of your bids, and used their feedback rating and written reviews as one of the influencing factors when selecting a contractor?

If you've had a good experience, leave a great review, list what you liked about the contractor and even what you didn't. This will help others select a contractor for their job based on your findings.

If you've had a horrible experience with your contractor, it's your responsibility to leave a negative review and list exactly what went wrong to prevent others from making the same mistake you did. Be honest and clear. The contractor may well respond to your comment, so unfair claims on your part will be pointed out. If you create a simple and clear response highlighting where he or she failed to meet your expectations, you'll be assisting others as they select contractors for their projects.

Remember, if you've taken the jump, have outsourced a task, and now have the knowledge required to make a more educated decision, it's your responsibility to help others out. A new user who is just starting out may well gain huge value from your review when selecting his or her first contractor. Leaving a review is a simple way of returning the favor and will add value for your fellow co-employers.

CHAPTER 12:
PITFALLS AND CHALLENGES

PAYMENT SCAMS

No doubt when you think about outsourcing, you think about how hard it can be or what's likely to go wrong. There are many stories about people getting ripped off, having nothing delivered, or even just having contractors go quiet and no longer be contactable.

Honestly, this does happen. In fact, it can happen quite a lot. So you need to consider how you might mitigate these risks early on.

When you are defining milestones, communicate that at the completion of each milestone, your contractor will release a portion of the overall payment via escrow. This will enable you to keep the contractor focused while drip-feeding his or her fee over time. This is perhaps the safest option.

If the contractor requests a prepayment, it will generally be a minimal fee, for example, 5% in advance, 65% split up over a number of milestones, and 30% at the completion and delivery of the final product.

Always remember that the contractor doing the work for you is likely depending on this work to feed his or her family. In the event that you are completely unsatisfied with the quality of work delivered, you might be justified to decline payment to the contractor. If you are refusing payment, ensure you reference the appropriate terms of use when explaining this to the contractor. Another good move is to contact the outsourcing platform and inform them of your situation. If you provided a fair, accurate and detailed brief, you'll have a reasonably strong case and the contractor will struggle to argue against you.

QUICK TIP

In the event that you don't pay, you should note that each of the outsourcing platforms will have a listed terms of use you've already accepted. If the contractor has a case, he or she may well take action against you.

In order to ultimately mitigate the risk of a payment conflict, you might utilize an escrow service, which will hold money, display the balance to the contractor, and allow you to control when this is released. In this case, you'll have the most control over when the contractor is paid, and they'll have the confidence in knowing that the money is available.

INTELLECTUAL PROPERTY

People often express concern about the reliability of using outsourced suppliers. They are worried about their website code or template leaking out or being reused. They are worried about the contractor stealing their idea or doing something new with it. They could even be concerned about their contractor contacting their competition with insider information.

Ultimately, if you're so concerned about IP (Intellectual Property) that it's preventing you from wanting to even start looking at outsourcing, then outsourcing probably isn't for you. If you've got a project that is so top secret and have an idea that the world is desperate to learn about, then let's face it, you need to have a team you can lock in a room and prevent from accessing the outside world.

Some people get their contractors to sign non-disclosure and non-compete agreements, but in most cases, these won't achieve much, if anything. If contractors want to run out and create their own version of your product, they probably will, and there is generally very little you can do.

This isn't all doom and gloom. In truth, once you launch your site, if it's as amazing as you think it is, it is probably going to be copied anyway (no, really, it's going to be copied). There are dodgy people all over the world duplicating websites every day to make a quick buck. As a result, it doesn't pay to get too worried about a contractor stealing your work. Focus instead on getting your best possible product to market as quickly as possible.

If you do want to outsource but need a little more confidence, you can request your contractor sign an agreement that limits what he or she can do with the information you provide. Whether or not it would be worth taking action in the event that something goes wrong is, of course, up to you.

CHAPTER 13:
RESOURCES

OUTSOURCING SITES

www.elance.com
www.odesk.com
www.freelancer.com
www.vworker.com
www.fancyhands.com
www.taskrabbit.com
www.getfriday.com
www.yourmaninindia.com
www.remoteworkmate.com
www.fiverr.com

TOOLS THAT MIGHT HELP

Meetings online

www.gotomeeting.com
www.skype.com

Domain name registrars and website hosting

www.bluehost.com
www.crazydomains.com.au
www.hostgator.com
www.hover.com
www.godaddy.com
www.leandomainsearch.com
www.rackspace.com

Content Management Systems (CMS)

www.wordpress.org
www.magento.com
www.joomla.org
www.businesscatalyst.com

CHAPTER 14:
BONUS

HOW I GOT THIS FAR...

After getting this far, I thought it might be worth letting you know how I got this book to market.

First of all, the logo you see on the front cover of this book and on the website from which you downloaded it were created via an outsourced contractor. I simply put up a very basic brief and had 17 proposals the next day, ranging from $40 and $250. I selected this particular logo from a contractor based in India. The contractor's hourly rate is $10/hour; the bid for the total job was $60. The contractor also had a great portfolio, which was hard to pass by.

The website that you possibly purchased this book from, was created with templates I purchased from www.themeforest.net and www.optimizepress.com. Neither were above $100.

While not traditional outsourcing, it's worth a mention that after purchasing my hosting, URL and the template, I contracted (via Elance) a web system admin for 2 hours to set up my Google Apps (email) and Google Analytics, install Wordpress and configure a basic homepage. Completing this amount of work would have taken me away from work for a whole day, whereas I was able to get the complete job finished by a web expert in just a couple of hours.

The final book you're reading now was even proofread and edited by an American author I found on Elance. She was able to read, review and make recommendations for just over $70. The audio recording of this book was outsourced to an experienced American voice actor for $400.

THE NEXT STEP

Shoot me an email to matt@mattkelly.com.au if you've read this far, I'll email you a bonus free gift!

NOTES